I ♥ COFFEE COLORING BOOK

this book belongs to:

....

COPYRIGHT

All rights reserved.
No part of this book may be reproduced in any form
without written permission of the copyright owners.
Copyright © 2020 Maia Laurel.

INSTRUCTIONS

1. Use the swatch page to test out your favorite color combinations!

2. Take time out each day for one month to complete the 30 day coffee doodle challenge.

3. Get creative and enjoy! Use this book to de-stress by combining your favourite hobby with some relaxing and calming down time and clear a busy mind.

4. Carefully remove your favorite finished pages to gift, frame or just stick on your fridge!

SWATCH PAGE

TEST YOUR COLOR COMBINATIONS ON THESE SWATCH PATCHES!

... AND ALSO ON THESE COFFEE DOODLES!

SCRIBBLE TEST PAGE

TEST OUT YOUR FANCIEST PENS AND PRACTICE FOR YOUR DOODLE CHALLENGE ON THIS PAGE!

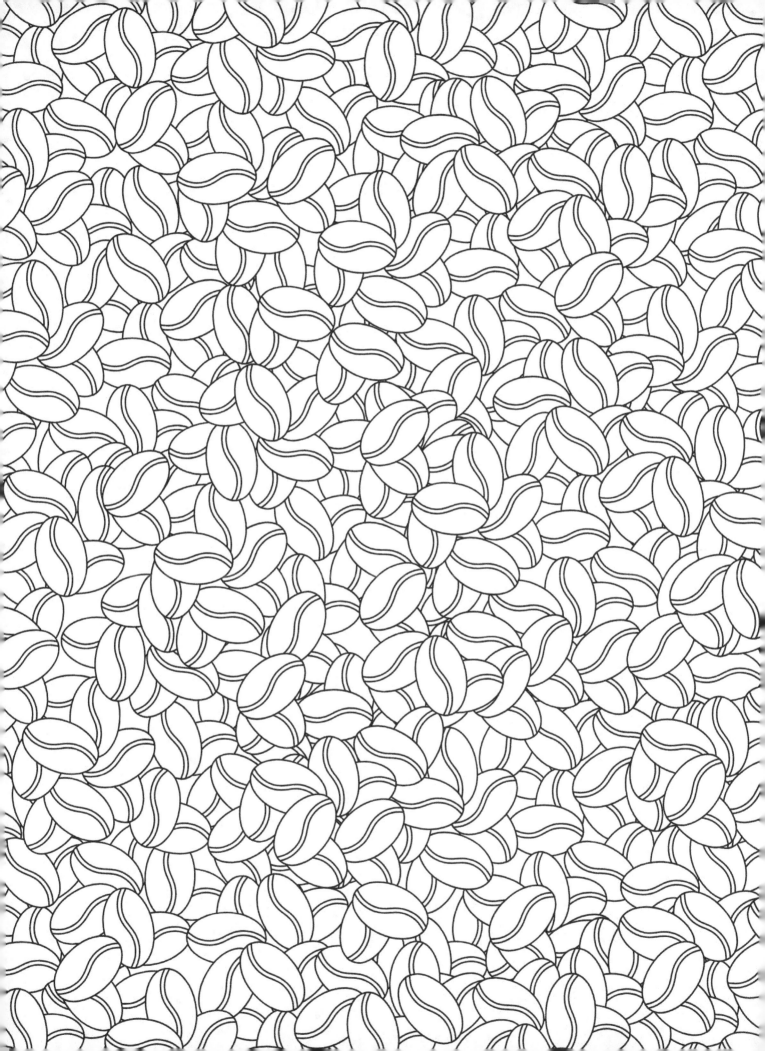

NOT ALL WHO WANDER ARE LOST

SOME ARE JUST LOOKING FOR COFFEE.

I LIKE BIG CUPS & I CANNOT LIE

HOW DO I FEEL WITHOUT COFFEE?

☹

DEPRESSO.

HOW DO I FEEL WITHOUT COFFEE?

☹

DEPRESSO.

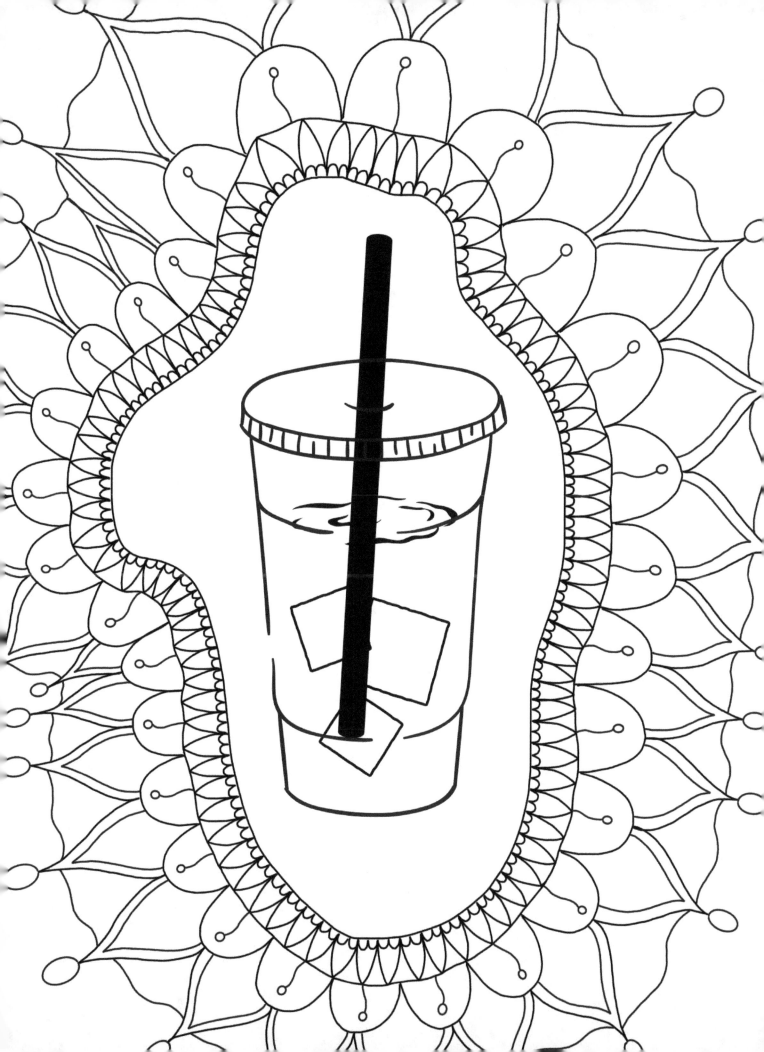

I MUST GET UP. MY COFFEE NEEDS ME.

I MUST GET UP. MY COFFEE NEEDS ME.

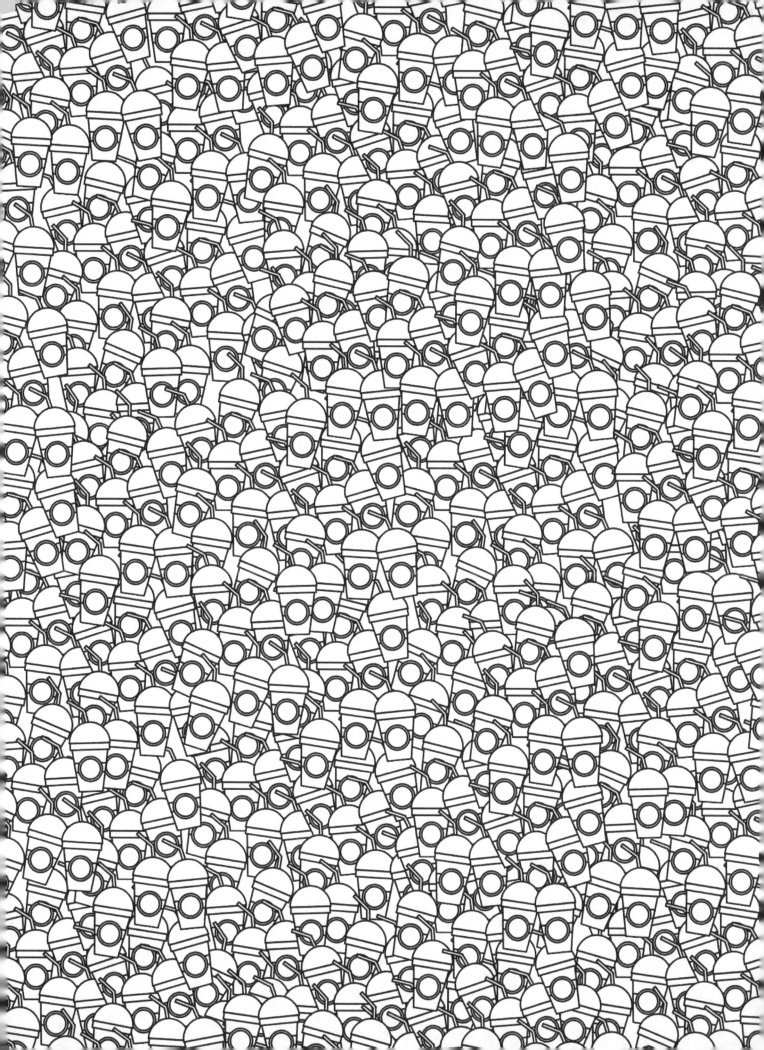

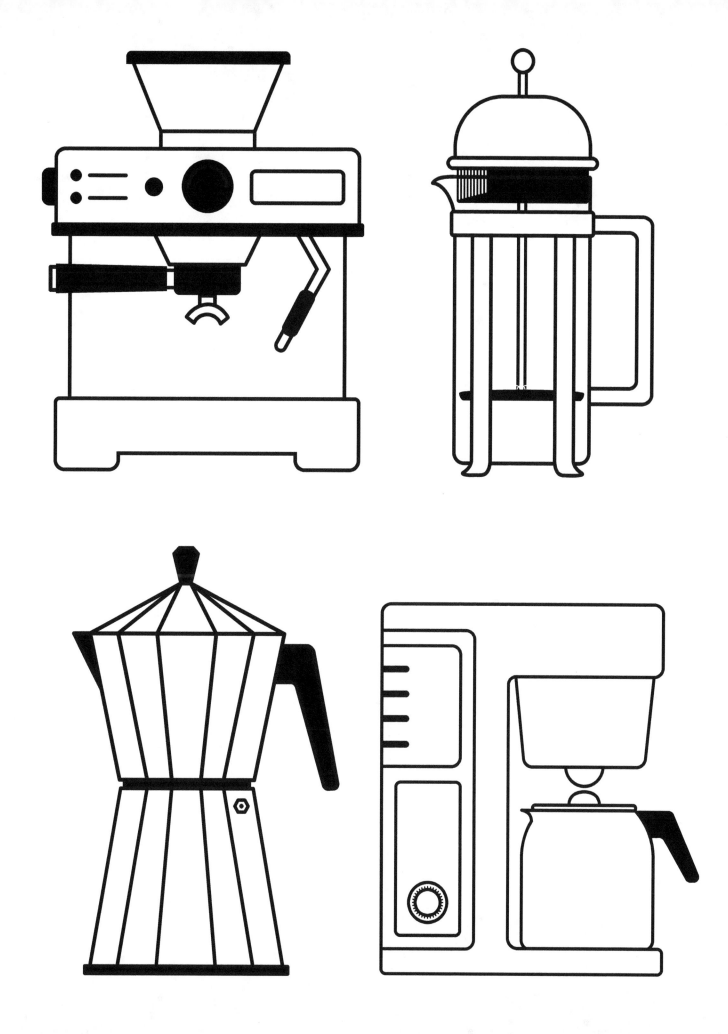

DOODLE A DAY / 30 DAY DOODLE CHALLENGE

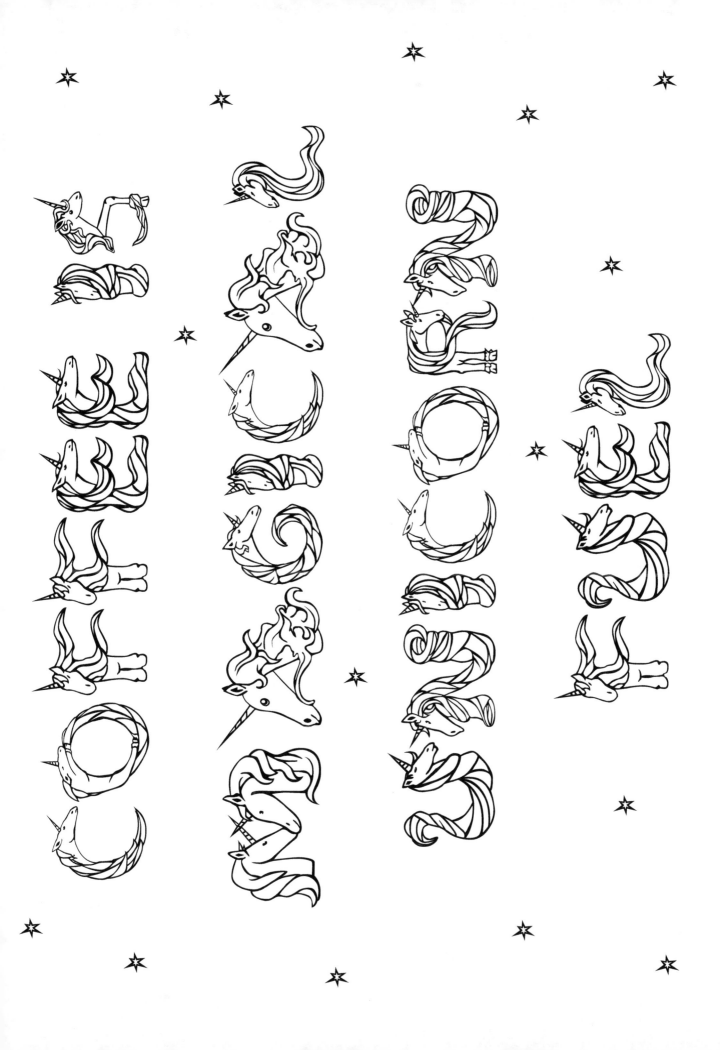

YOU CALL IT
COFFEE.
I CALL IT MY
EMOTIONAL
SUPPORT
BEVERAGE.

- americano
- AFFOGATO
- JAVA
- crema
- dalgona
- COLD BREW
- MOCHA
- DARK ROAST
- iced
- RISTRETTO
- AROMA
- BARISTA
- doppio
- CORTADO
- FLAT WHITE
- espresso
- french press
- MACCHIATO
- pour over

SCRAP PAPER

SCRAP PAPER

SCRAP PAPER

CPSIA information can be obtained
at www.ICGtesting.com
Printed in the USA
LVHW020312120723
752250LV00026B/391